Table of Content

THE
POWER
OF
PRAYER

Unlocking Heaven's Power
Through Intimacy With God

DR. GREG WOOD

Dedication

To every believer who longs for a deeper walk with God.

To the weary intercessor who feels unseen.

To the faithful grandmother who still prays for her prodigal child.

To the pastor who cries out for revival in his city.

To the young disciple just learning to pray.

This book is for you. May you discover that prayer is not a burden but a blessing, not a duty but a delight, not a ritual but a relationship.

And most of all—this book is dedicated to the glory of the One who hears every whisper, catches every tear, and answers every prayer—our Heavenly Father.

Acknowledgements

First and foremost, I thank God, who in His mercy has given me both the privilege and responsibility to write on the subject of prayer. Without Him, these pages would be empty words. With Him, they carry life and truth.

I am deeply grateful to the countless men and women of faith whose lives of prayer have inspired me. The saints of Scripture—Abraham, Hannah, Daniel, David, and Paul—have been teachers across the centuries. The intercessors of history—such as George Müller, Rees Howells, and the Moravians—have shown what God can do through persistent prayer.

To the pastors, mentors, and spiritual leaders who have poured into me—thank you for modeling lives saturated in prayer. To family and friends who encouraged me to press into God's presence, your support has been invaluable.

To Kingsway Fellowship International of Des Moines, Iowa for over 50 years of support and unconditional love.

Finally, to every reader of this book: thank you for opening your heart to the call of prayer. My prayer is that these words will stir a fire in you that will not go out.

Preface

Prayer is the most powerful, yet often most neglected, gift God has given His children. It is the means by which heaven touches earth, the weak connect with the Almighty, and the ordinary are empowered for extraordinary living.

This book is not intended to be a manual of formulas or mechanical techniques. Rather, it is a journey—a call to intimacy with God through prayer. Each chapter explores a different dimension of prayer, drawing from Scripture, history, and practical examples, while also offering reflection questions to guide personal growth.

The pages ahead are written in a teaching and devotional style, with the hope that they can be read both privately and in small groups, in quiet reflection or in lively discussion. Whether you are just beginning to explore prayer or have walked with God for many years, there is always more to discover in the endless depths of His presence.

My hope is simple: that this book would ignite in you a passion for prayer—a hunger to know God more deeply, to trust Him more fully, and to see His power manifested in your life, your family, your church, and your nation.

As you read, may the Spirit of God draw you into fresh encounters with the Living God. And may your prayer life become not an occasional act, but the heartbeat of your walk with Christ.

Dr. Greg Wood

THE POWER OF PRAYER

Unlocking Heaven's Power Through Intimacy With God

by

Dr. Greg Wood
First Edition – 2025

Chapter 1 – What is Prayer?

The Foundation of Prayer

Prayer is one of the greatest mysteries of the Christian life. On the surface, it seems so simple—just words spoken from the heart. And yet, at the same time, it is one of the most profound acts a believer can ever engage in. Through prayer, the finite touches the Infinite. Through prayer, earth reaches heaven. Through prayer, weak human beings connect with the Almighty God.

Prayer is not optional for the believer; it is essential. Just as oxygen is necessary for physical life, prayer is the breath of spiritual life. Without prayer, the Christian faith becomes dry, mechanical, and powerless. But with prayer, the believer's life is infused with strength, direction, and intimacy with God.

When Jesus walked the earth, His disciples could have asked Him to teach them many things. They could have said, "Lord, teach us how to preach," or "Teach us how to work miracles." But instead, they said, *"Lord, teach us to pray"* (Luke 11:1). They recognized that prayer was the source of His power.

Defining Prayer

What is prayer? At its simplest, prayer is **communication with God**. It is speaking, listening, and communing with Him. But to define it only as communication is too shallow, for prayer is more than words—it is fellowship.

- **Prayer is conversation** – We talk with God as a child talks with a loving father.
- **Prayer is communion** – We share in the life of God, experiencing His presence.
- **Prayer is covenant** – It is rooted in relationship and promise, not ritual.

Jesus emphasized this when He taught His disciples to pray by beginning with *"Our Father which art in heaven"* (Matthew 6:9). Prayer starts with relationship, not with requests.

One writer described prayer as "the key in the hand of faith to unlock heaven's storehouse." Another said, "Prayer is the slender nerve that moves the muscle of omnipotence." Prayer is both simple enough for a child to do, yet deep enough to occupy the most mature saint for a lifetime.

Biblical Examples of Prayer

The Bible is filled with stories of men and women whose lives were marked by prayer.

- **Abraham** interceded for Sodom, negotiating with God for the lives of the righteous (Genesis 18:23–33).
- **Moses** prayed on the mountain and God spared Israel from destruction (Exodus 32:11–14).
- **Hannah** poured out her heart in prayer, and God answered with the gift of a son, Samuel (1 Samuel 1:10–20).
- **David** prayed with honesty and passion in the Psalms, showing us how to bring our emotions before God.
- **Daniel** prayed faithfully three times a day, even when threatened with death, and God delivered him from the lions (Daniel 6:10–23).
- **Jesus** Himself withdrew often to pray. His prayer life was the wellspring of His ministry (Mark 1:35; Luke 6:12).

These examples remind us that prayer is not reserved for prophets and priests, but for every believer.

Why Prayer Matters

Why should we pray? Some might ask, "If God knows everything, why pray at all?" But Scripture shows us several important reasons:

1. **God Commands It** – *"Pray without ceasing."* (1 Thessalonians 5:17) Prayer is not optional—it is an instruction from the Lord.
2. **We Need It** – Just as the body needs food and water, the spirit needs prayer to stay alive and strong.
3. **It Changes Us** – Prayer softens our hearts, aligns us with God's will, and builds faith.
4. **It Moves Heaven** – James 5:16 says, *"The effectual fervent prayer of a righteous man availeth much."* Prayer truly makes a difference.
5. **It Glorifies God** – When we pray, we acknowledge our dependence on Him, and He receives the glory when prayers are answered.

Illustrations of Prayer

Think of a soldier in battle. His radio connects him to headquarters, where reinforcements, instructions, and supplies can be sent. If the radio is silent, the soldier is isolated, vulnerable, and powerless. Prayer is that radio line between us and the Captain of our salvation.

Or consider a marriage. A husband and wife who never speak will drift apart. Communication is the lifeline of relationship. Prayer is the believer's communication with God—without it, our intimacy with Him suffers.

The Two-Way Nature of Prayer

Many think prayer is only talking to God, but it is also listening. Samuel said, *"Speak, Lord, for thy servant heareth"* (1 Samuel 3:9). Elijah heard God's voice not in the wind, the earthquake, or the fire, but in a still small voice (1 Kings 19:11–12).

If we only speak and never listen, we turn prayer into a monologue. But true prayer is dialogue. We must quiet our hearts and listen for His voice through His Word, His Spirit, and His gentle impressions.

Prayer as Transformation

One of the greatest truths about prayer is that while we often want God to change circumstances, He often uses prayer to change us.

- Moses came down from the mountain after forty days of prayer, and his face shone with God's glory (Exodus 34:29).
- Jesus prayed in Gethsemane, and though the cup did not pass, He emerged strengthened to fulfill His mission (Luke 22:42–43).
- Paul prayed for his thorn to be removed, but God answered with grace sufficient to endure (2 Corinthians 12:7–9).

Prayer transforms us into the likeness of Christ.

Reflection & Study Questions

1. In your own words, how would you define prayer?
2. Why do you think the disciples asked Jesus to teach them to pray, rather than to preach or perform miracles?
3. Which biblical figure's prayer life inspires you most—Abraham, Hannah, Daniel, or another?
4. Have you ever experienced prayer changing *you* more than it changed your situation? Reflect on that moment.
5. Take 15 minutes this week to practice silent listening prayer. What do you sense God speaking to you?

Chapter 2 – Why Prayer is Powerful

The Source of Power in Prayer

Prayer is powerful—not because of the one who prays, but because of the One who hears. The strength of prayer is not in eloquence, length, or volume. The strength of prayer is in the God who sits on the throne of heaven and bends His ear toward His children.

James 5:16 declares: *"The effectual fervent prayer of a righteous man availeth much."* This means prayer works. It accomplishes things. It shakes the heavens and transforms the earth. Why? Because prayer is not human effort—it is divine partnership. When we pray, we connect our weakness to God's omnipotence, our limitations to His unlimited power.

The Authority of the Believer in Prayer

One reason prayer is powerful is that Jesus gave His followers authority in His name. In John 14:13–14, He said:

"And whatsoever ye shall ask in my name, that will I do, that the Father may be glorified in the Son. If ye shall ask any thing in my name, I will do it."

To pray in Jesus' name is not a mere formula at the end of our prayers. It is standing in the authority of Christ, as if Jesus Himself were making the request. When a believer prays in faith, under the authority of Christ, heaven responds.

Biblical Proof of Prayer's Power

Throughout Scripture, prayer changed lives, nations, and history:

- **Elijah** prayed and the heavens withheld rain for three and a half years. Then he prayed again and the heavens poured forth rain (1 Kings 17–18; James 5:17–18).
- **Joshua** prayed, and the sun stood still until Israel defeated their enemies (Joshua 10:12–14).
- **Hezekiah** prayed for healing, and God added fifteen years to

his life (2 Kings 20:1–6).
- **The early church** prayed while Peter was in prison, and an angel broke his chains and set him free (Acts 12:5–11).

Prayer not only changed situations—it altered destinies. It closed the mouths of lions, opened prison doors, healed the sick, raised the dead, and turned nations back to God.

Illustrations of Prayer's Effectiveness

Think of prayer like the electrical cord plugged into a power outlet. The lamp itself has no power, but when it connects to the source, light shines in the darkness. Prayer is that cord—it connects us to God's power supply.

Another illustration is that of a key. A locked door can be intimidating, but prayer is the key that unlocks it. Behind the door are answers, provision, healing, peace, and breakthrough. Without prayer, the door remains closed. With prayer, God opens what no man can shut (Revelation 3:7).

Testimonies of Prayer's Power in History

History also testifies to the power of prayer:

- In **1857**, Jeremiah Lanphier began a noonday prayer meeting in New York City with just six people. Within six months, 10,000 businessmen were gathering daily for prayer. This prayer revival swept across America, leading to thousands of conversions.
- During **World War II**, Rees Howells and a group of intercessors in Wales prayed fervently for the defeat of Nazi Germany. Many believe their prayers turned the tide of key battles.
- In **the Hebrides Revival** (1949–1952), two elderly sisters prayed faithfully for God to move on their island. Their prayers sparked a revival that transformed the community, with bars

closing, churches filling, and countless souls saved.

These stories remind us: prayer is not a weak gesture—it is a mighty weapon.

What Makes Prayer Powerful?

1. **Prayer Invites God's Presence** – God inhabits the praises of His people (Psalm 22:3), and He draws near when His children pray.
2. **Prayer Releases God's Power** – Heaven responds to prayer with signs, wonders, and miracles.
3. **Prayer Aligns Us With God's Will** – Jesus prayed, *"Not my will, but thine be done."* Prayer aligns our desires with His perfect plan.
4. **Prayer Builds Our Faith** – Every answered prayer strengthens our trust in God for the future.
5. **Prayer Defeats the Enemy** – Prayer is part of our spiritual armor (Ephesians 6:18), a weapon that brings victory over darkness.

The Difference Between Empty Words and Powerful Prayer

Not all prayer is powerful. Jesus warned against vain repetitions (Matthew 6:7). Empty words, without faith or relationship, do not move the heart of God. Powerful prayer is:

- **Sincere** – Coming from a genuine heart.
- **Faith-filled** – Rooted in God's promises.
- **Persistent** – Continuing even when answers delay.
- **Aligned** – Submitted to God's will.

The Pharisee in Luke 18 prayed proudly and received nothing. The tax collector humbled himself and was justified. Power in prayer comes not from pride, but from humility and faith.

Reflection & Study Questions

1. What is the true source of power in prayer?
2. How does praying "in Jesus' name" change the way you approach prayer?
3. Which biblical example of answered prayer inspires you most, and why?
4. Can you recall a time when prayer changed a situation in your life—or changed you?
5. What adjustments could you make to move your prayer life from ritual to power-filled relationship?

Chapter 3 – The Prayer Life of Jesus

Jesus: Our Perfect Model of Prayer

If there is one life that demonstrates the power, purpose, and practice of prayer, it is the life of Jesus Christ. Though He was the eternal Son of God—equal with the Father—He consistently modeled a life of dependence on prayer. His ministry on earth was not fueled by human ability but by communion with His Father.

The disciples recognized this. They witnessed Him healing the sick, casting out demons, raising the dead, and preaching with authority. Yet they did not say, *"Lord, teach us to heal"* or *"Teach us to preach."* Instead, they said, *"Lord, teach us to pray"* (Luke 11:1). They knew His secret was not in His methods, but in His prayer life.

Jesus Prayed Early and Often

Mark 1:35 gives us a glimpse: *"And in the morning, rising up a great while before day, he went out, and departed into a solitary place, and there prayed."*

Before the day began, before the demands of ministry, Jesus prioritized prayer. The busier He became, the more He withdrew to pray. This stands in stark contrast to how many believers today abandon prayer when life grows hectic. Jesus shows us that the greater the responsibility, the greater the need for prayer.

Luke 5:16 says, *"And he withdrew himself into the wilderness, and prayed."* Prayer was not an occasional activity for Jesus; it was His lifestyle.

Key Moments of Prayer in Jesus' Life

1. **At His Baptism** – As He prayed, the heavens opened and the Spirit descended like a dove (Luke 3:21–22). Prayer ushered in the empowerment for His ministry.
2. **Before Choosing the Twelve** – Jesus spent an entire night in

prayer before selecting His apostles (Luke 6:12–13). Major decisions were bathed in prayer.

3. **Before Feeding the Multitudes** – He blessed the loaves and fish in prayer, and they multiplied (John 6:11). Prayer turned scarcity into abundance.

4. **At Lazarus' Tomb** – He prayed before raising Lazarus, showing that miracles flow out of communion with the Father (John 11:41–42).

5. **At His Transfiguration** – As He prayed, His appearance changed and glory radiated from Him (Luke 9:28–29). Prayer revealed His divine nature.

6. **In Gethsemane** – Facing the cross, He prayed with such intensity that His sweat became drops of blood (Luke 22:44). Prayer gave Him strength to surrender to the Father's will.

7. **On the Cross** – His final words were prayers: *"Father, forgive them..."* (Luke 23:34), *"My God, my God, why hast thou forsaken me?"* (Matthew 27:46), and *"Father, into thy hands I commend my spirit"* (Luke 23:46). Even in death, He prayed.

The Secret of Jesus' Power

Every miracle, every sermon, every decision flowed from His prayer life. His authority was rooted in His intimacy with the Father.

John 5:19 records His words: *"The Son can do nothing of himself, but what he seeth the Father do."* How did He see what the Father was doing? Through prayerful communion.

Lessons from Jesus' Prayer Life

1. **Prayer Must Be a Priority** – Jesus prayed early in the morning, at night, in solitude, in public, before meals, before miracles, and in crisis. He showed us prayer must be constant.

2. **Prayer Prepares Us for Purpose** – Before great decisions or challenges, Jesus prayed. Likewise, we should seek God's

guidance before we step into major moments of life.

3. **Prayer Sustains Us in Suffering** – In Gethsemane, Jesus prayed not to escape the cross but to endure it. Prayer gave Him strength to submit.

4. **Prayer is Rooted in Relationship** – Jesus always addressed God as Father. He prayed not as a servant to a master but as a Son to His beloved Father.

An Illustration

Imagine a violinist playing in a grand concert hall. To the audience, the performance is flawless. But what they do not see is the hours spent tuning the instrument before stepping on stage. Without tuning, the music would be discordant. Prayer was the "tuning" of Jesus' life—aligning Him with the will of the Father so that every act and word was in harmony with heaven.

Modern Examples of Following Jesus' Model

- **John Wesley**, founder of Methodism, rose daily at 4 a.m. to spend two hours in prayer. He said, "God does nothing except in answer to prayer."
- **Smith Wigglesworth**, the evangelist known for miraculous healings, rarely prayed more than 30 minutes—but he never went more than 30 minutes without praying.
- **Mother Teresa** spent hours in prayer daily, drawing strength to serve the poorest of the poor.

Each of these leaders mirrored Jesus' rhythm of prayer and power.

Reflection & Study Questions

1. Why do you think Jesus, though fully God, still needed to pray constantly?
2. Which key moment of Jesus' prayer life speaks most to your

current season?

3. How can you make prayer a daily priority, as Jesus did?

4. What major decisions in your life right now need to be bathed in prayer?

5. Take 20 minutes this week to pray following Jesus' example—starting with worship, listening, surrendering, and then making your requests.

Chapter 4 – The Holy Spirit and Prayer

The Role of the Holy Spirit in Prayer

The Christian life is impossible without the Holy Spirit. He is our Comforter, Teacher, and Guide. When it comes to prayer, He is our greatest helper. Paul writes in Romans 8:26–27:

"Likewise the Spirit also helpeth our infirmities: for we know not what we should pray for as we ought: but the Spirit itself maketh intercession for us with groanings which cannot be uttered. And he that searcheth the hearts knoweth what is the mind of the Spirit, because he maketh intercession for the saints according to the will of God."

This means that prayer is not something we must carry out in our own weakness. The Spirit comes alongside us, guiding, strengthening, and even praying through us when words fail.

Our Weakness in Prayer

Paul admits, *"We know not what we should pray for as we ought."* How true this is!

- Sometimes we don't know **what** to pray for. Our understanding is limited.
- Sometimes we don't know **how** to pray. Our words seem inadequate.
- Sometimes we don't know **when** or **why** things happen as they do.

But here lies the good news: we are not left to our own limitations. The Spirit intercedes with us and through us. He takes our broken words, our tears, our silence, and carries them before the throne of God.

Praying in the Spirit

Paul exhorts believers in Ephesians 6:18: *"Praying always with all prayer and supplication in the Spirit..."*

To "pray in the Spirit" is more than simply saying prayers. It means allowing the Holy Spirit to inspire, direct, and energize our prayers. This can include:

- **Praying with understanding** – as the Spirit gives insight into God's Word.
- **Praying with guidance** – when the Spirit burdens us for a person, nation, or situation we hadn't thought of.
- **Praying in tongues** – as the Spirit gives utterance beyond our natural language (1 Corinthians 14:2).
- **Praying with boldness** – as the Spirit fills us with courage to ask in faith.

The Spirit's Intercession

There are moments when our souls are so heavy that words fail. In those times, the Spirit groans within us, interceding with cries too deep for expression. This is prayer at its purest—where the Spirit Himself pleads on our behalf.

In Gethsemane, Jesus prayed in agony, and Scripture says an angel strengthened Him (Luke 22:43). In a similar way, the Spirit strengthens us when prayer feels like a burden too heavy to bear.

The Spirit and Spiritual Warfare

Prayer is not only communion with God—it is also confrontation with the enemy. That is why Paul includes prayer in the armor of God (Ephesians 6:18). Just as soldiers rely on strategy and intelligence from their commanders, believers rely on the Spirit to guide them in spiritual battle.

The Spirit may direct us to pray against demonic oppression, to intercede for revival, or to stand in the gap for someone under attack. Spirit-led prayer is warfare prayer.

Historical and Modern Testimonies

- **The Moravians** in the 1700s began a prayer watch that continued day and night for over 100 years. Spirit-led prayer birthed a missionary movement that touched the world.
- **Evan Roberts**, a young Welsh miner, was so filled with the Spirit in prayer that the 1904 Welsh Revival spread like fire, bringing 100,000 souls to Christ in months.
- Countless believers today testify of moments when the Spirit led them to pray for someone at just the right time—only to discover that person was in urgent need.

The Spirit knows what we do not know, sees what we cannot see, and moves us to pray accordingly.

Illustration

Prayer without the Spirit is like a sailboat without wind. The sails may be up, the boat may be in the water, but without wind it remains motionless. When the Holy Spirit fills the sails, the boat moves with power and direction. In the same way, the Spirit is the wind of prayer, carrying us forward into God's will.

How to Cultivate Spirit-Led Prayer

1. **Yield to the Spirit** – Begin prayer by inviting the Spirit to guide your words and thoughts.
2. **Pray Scripture** – The Spirit always aligns with God's Word; praying Scripture ensures Spirit-filled prayer.
3. **Listen** – Leave silence for the Spirit to impress burdens or insights on your heart.
4. **Pray in Tongues (if gifted)** – Allow the Spirit to bypass your limitations and pray mysteries according to God's will.
5. **Stay Sensitive** – Be ready to pray anytime the Spirit nudges you

Reflection & Study Questions

1. What does it mean to you that the Spirit "helps our infirmities" in prayer?
2. Can you recall a time when you didn't know how to pray, but sensed the Spirit interceding through you?
3. How can you grow in "praying in the Spirit" daily?
4. In what ways does Spirit-led prayer equip us for spiritual warfare?
5. This week, set aside one prayer time specifically to invite the Spirit to lead your intercession. Write down what He shows you.

Chapter 5 – Hindrances to Prayer

The Reality of Prayer Barriers

While prayer is powerful, many believers experience seasons when their prayers seem ineffective or hindered. They pray but feel as though the heavens are brass and their words bounce back. The Bible is clear: there are obstacles that can block, delay, or weaken prayer.

Just as a clogged pipe restricts the flow of water, certain attitudes, sins, and conditions can restrict the flow of God's answers. To pray effectively, we must understand these hindrances and remove them.

1. Unconfessed Sin

Psalm 66:18 declares: *"If I regard iniquity in my heart, the Lord will not hear me."*

Sin creates distance between us and God. Though He is merciful, God calls us to repentance before He responds. A rebellious heart cannot expect divine answers.

- **Example:** In Isaiah 59:2, God told Israel, *"Your iniquities have separated between you and your God, and your sins have hid his face from you, that he will not hear."*
- **Application:** Before we ask God for blessings, we must first ask Him for cleansing (1 John 1:9).

2. Unforgiveness

Jesus taught in Mark 11:25: *"When ye stand praying, forgive, if ye have ought against any: that your Father also which is in heaven may forgive you your trespasses."*

Bitterness and unforgiveness hinder prayer because they grieve the Holy Spirit. God cannot release His mercy to us if we withhold mercy from others.

- **Illustration:** A believer who clings to unforgiveness is like a person trying to drink from a well while holding the lid tightly closed. Release opens the flow.

3. Wrong Motives

James 4:3 says: *"Ye ask, and receive not, because ye ask amiss, that ye may consume it upon your lusts."*

Prayers driven by selfish ambition, greed, or pride are hindered. Prayer is not about manipulating God to fulfill our desires, but aligning with His will.

- **Example:** The Pharisee in Luke 18 prayed proudly, exalting himself, while the humble tax collector was justified. God resists the proud but gives grace to the humble (James 4:6).

4. Doubt and Unbelief

Faith is essential in prayer. Hebrews 11:6 reminds us: *"Without faith it is impossible to please him."* When we pray without believing, our prayers lose power.

James 1:6–7 warns that the one who doubts is like a wave tossed by the sea: *"Let not that man think that he shall receive any thing of the Lord."*

- **Application:** Faith anchors prayer in God's promises. Unbelief cuts the anchor line and leaves us drifting.

5. Neglect of God's Word

Prayer and the Word go hand in hand. John 15:7 says: *"If ye abide in me, and my words abide in you, ye shall ask what ye will, and it shall be done unto you."*

A prayer life disconnected from Scripture becomes shallow. When God's Word fills our hearts, it fuels faith and aligns our requests with His will.

- **Illustration:** A fire burns brighter when fed with wood. Likewise, prayer burns stronger when fueled with Scripture.

6. Broken Relationships

1 Peter 3:7 instructs husbands to honor their wives, *"that your prayers be not hindered."* Disharmony in relationships can affect our spiritual connection with God.

Jesus also said in Matthew 5:23–24 that if we bring our gift to the altar and remember a brother has something against us, we should reconcile first. God values unity and reconciliation.

7. Distractions and Prayerlessness

Sometimes the greatest hindrance to prayer is simply neglect. We are so busy with life, technology, and worries that we fail to pray.

- **Example:** The disciples in Gethsemane could not stay awake to pray. Jesus warned, *"Watch and pray, that ye enter not into temptation"* (Matthew 26:41).
- **Application:** Neglecting prayer leaves us spiritually weak and vulnerable.

Removing Hindrances

The good news is that God has given us a way to deal with every hindrance:

1. **Repent of sin** – Confess and turn away (1 John 1:9).
2. **Forgive others** – Release offenses and choose love (Colossians 3:13).
3. **Check motives** – Align desires with God's glory (Matthew 6:33).
4. **Strengthen faith** – Build faith through the Word and testimonies (Romans 10:17).
5. **Abide in Scripture** – Let God's Word guide prayers (John

15:7).

6. **Seek reconciliation** – Pursue peace with others (Hebrews 12:14).
7. **Discipline yourself** – Develop a consistent rhythm of prayer.

Illustration

Imagine trying to drive a powerful sports car but leaving the parking brake on. No matter how strong the engine is, the car struggles to move. In the same way, hindrances in our lives act like spiritual brakes. When removed, prayer flows freely, and the power of God is fully released.

Reflection & Study Questions

1. Which of these hindrances—sin, unforgiveness, wrong motives, doubt, neglect, broken relationships, or distraction—do you struggle with most?
2. Have you ever noticed a season where prayer felt blocked? What was the cause?
3. How can you make confession and forgiveness a regular part of your prayer life?
4. What steps can you take to strengthen your faith and remove unbelief in prayer?
5. This week, ask the Holy Spirit to reveal any hindrance in your life. Write down what He shows you and take steps to clear it.

Chapter 6 – Praying with Faith

Faith: The Foundation of Effective Prayer

Prayer without faith is like a bird without wings—it cannot rise. Faith is the essential ingredient that gives prayer its power. Hebrews 11:6 says: *"But without faith it is impossible to please him: for he that cometh to God must believe that he is, and that he is a rewarder of them that diligently seek him."*

Faith is not wishful thinking or blind optimism. Faith is confident trust in the character, promises, and power of God. When we pray with faith, we are not hoping vaguely that something *might* happen; we are standing firmly on the assurance that God hears, God cares, and God answers.

The Prayer of Faith

James 5:15 declares: *"And the prayer of faith shall save the sick, and the Lord shall raise him up."* The "prayer of faith" is more than words—it is prayer infused with expectation, grounded in God's Word, and surrendered to His will.

Faith-filled prayer is:

1. **Confident in God's Nature** – Believing He is good, loving, and faithful.
2. **Rooted in God's Word** – Claiming promises He has already spoken.
3. **Persistent in God's Timing** – Trusting Him even when answers delay.
4. **Surrendered to God's Will** – Submitting, as Jesus prayed, *"Nevertheless not my will, but thine, be done."* (Luke 22:42).

Biblical Examples of Praying with Faith

- **Hannah** prayed for a son with tears and faith. She vowed to dedicate him to God, and Samuel was born (1 Samuel 1).

- **Elijah** prayed for rain after three years of drought. Though the sky was clear, he prayed persistently until a small cloud appeared (1 Kings 18:41–45).
- **The Centurion** in Matthew 8 believed Jesus could heal his servant with a word. Jesus marveled at his faith and granted his request.
- **The Woman with the Issue of Blood** believed if she could just touch Jesus' garment, she would be healed. Her faith drew power from Him (Mark 5:25–34).

Faith did not deny the reality of their problems. Hannah was barren, Elijah faced drought, the Centurion's servant was sick, and the woman was desperate. But they chose to see beyond circumstances to the greatness of God.

Overcoming Doubt in Prayer

Doubt is the enemy of faith. James 1:6–7 warns: *"But let him ask in faith, nothing wavering. For he that wavereth is like a wave of the sea driven with the wind and tossed. For let not that man think that he shall receive any thing of the Lord."*

How do we overcome doubt?

1. **Know God's Word** – Faith comes by hearing the Word (Romans 10:17).
2. **Remember God's Faithfulness** – Reflect on past answers to prayer.
3. **Reject Negative Voices** – Silence voices of fear and unbelief.
4. **Surround Yourself with Believers** – Agreement in prayer strengthens faith.
5. **Focus on God, Not Circumstances** – Peter walked on water until he looked at the storm (Matthew 14:30). Keep eyes on Jesus.

Faith in Delayed Answers

Sometimes the greatest test of faith is waiting. Abraham prayed for a son and waited 25 years. Joseph dreamed of greatness but endured betrayal and prison before seeing God's promise fulfilled.

Faith is not only believing for instant answers—it is trusting God's timing. Isaiah 40:31 reminds us: *"They that wait upon the Lord shall renew their strength."*

The Balance of Faith and God's Will

True faith is not demanding God to do what *we* want, but trusting Him to do what is best. Jesus modeled this in Gethsemane when He prayed, *"If it be possible, let this cup pass from me: nevertheless not as I will, but as thou wilt."* (Matthew 26:39).

Faith is not opposed to surrender. In fact, faith and surrender go hand in hand. Real faith believes that God's will is always better than ours.

Illustration

Think of a child jumping into a swimming pool into their father's arms. The child doesn't calculate water depth or analyze statistics of safety. They jump because they trust the father. That is faith-filled prayer: taking the leap because you know your Father will catch you.

Modern Testimonies of Faith in Prayer

- **George Müller**, who ran orphanages in 19th-century England, never asked people for money. Instead, he prayed in faith. Time after time, God provided food, clothes, and finances—sometimes at the very last minute. His journals recorded over 50,000 specific answered prayers.
- **Smith Wigglesworth**, known as the "apostle of faith," prayed boldly for the sick. He said, "God will pass over a thousand men to find one man who will believe Him." Countless testimonies of healing flowed from his prayer life.
- Everyday believers today testify of financial provision, healings,

restored marriages, and salvations through persistent, faith-filled prayer.

Practical Ways to Pray with Faith

1. **Anchor Every Prayer in Scripture** – Find a verse that matches your need and stand on it.
2. **Pray with Thanksgiving** – Thank God in advance as though the answer is already on the way (Philippians 4:6).
3. **Speak Life, Not Death** – Avoid canceling your prayer with words of doubt.
4. **Keep a Prayer Journal** – Record requests and testimonies to strengthen faith.
5. **Pray Boldly** – Approach the throne of grace with confidence (Hebrews 4:16).

Reflection & Study Questions

1. What does "the prayer of faith" mean to you personally?
2. Can you identify a time when God answered a prayer that required great faith from you?
3. Where in your life right now is God calling you to trust Him more deeply in prayer?
4. What promises from Scripture can you begin to pray over your current needs?
5. This week, choose one prayer request and pray with bold faith daily, thanking God in advance for the answer.

Chapter 7 – Different Types of Prayer

The Richness of Prayer

Prayer is not one-dimensional. Just as a healthy relationship involves conversation, listening, gratitude, requests, and even conflict resolution, prayer has many different expressions. The Bible reveals various types of prayer that, together, form a complete and balanced prayer life.

Paul wrote in Ephesians 6:18: *"Praying always with all prayer and supplication in the Spirit, and watching thereunto with all perseverance and supplication for all saints."* Notice the phrase **"all prayer"**—indicating there are different kinds of prayer, each serving a purpose.

The Prayer of Adoration (Worship)

Adoration is prayer focused not on what God can do for us, but on who He is. It is worship in prayer form.

- **Scripture:** *"Our Father which art in heaven, Hallowed be thy name."* (Matthew 6:9).
- **Example:** David often began his psalms by exalting God's greatness before bringing requests.
- **Application:** Begin your prayer time by lifting your eyes to God's majesty, holiness, and love.

Illustration: Adoration is like standing on a mountain peak, overwhelmed by the view. In the presence of God, our hearts swell with awe.

The Prayer of Confession

Confession acknowledges our sins and failures before God. It is the cleansing stream that restores fellowship with Him.

- **Scripture:** *"If we confess our sins, he is faithful and just to forgive us our sins, and to cleanse us from all unrighteousness."* (1 John

1:9).

- **Example:** David prayed in Psalm 51, confessing his sin with Bathsheba and asking for a clean heart.
- **Application:** Make confession a regular habit, not just when you feel guilty. Keep short accounts with God.

Illustration: Confession is like opening a window to let fresh air in, driving out the staleness.

The Prayer of Thanksgiving

Thanksgiving is expressing gratitude to God for His blessings, both big and small. Gratitude fuels joy and strengthens faith.

- **Scripture:** *"In every thing give thanks: for this is the will of God in Christ Jesus concerning you."* (1 Thessalonians 5:18).
- **Example:** Paul, even while imprisoned, gave thanks continually in his letters.
- **Application:** Keep a gratitude list. Thank God not only for answered prayers but also for daily mercies.

Illustration: Thanksgiving is like watering a plant. Gratitude causes the roots of faith to grow deeper.

The Prayer of Supplication (Asking)

Supplication is making personal requests before God. It is the most common form of prayer—bringing needs, desires, and petitions.

- **Scripture:** *"Be careful for nothing; but in every thing by prayer and supplication with thanksgiving let your requests be made known unto God."* (Philippians 4:6).
- **Example:** Hannah prayed earnestly for a child, and God granted her request.
- **Application:** Be specific in supplication. God invites us to ask boldly as children ask their father.

Illustration: Supplication is like a child bringing an empty cup to a fountain—expecting it to be filled.

The Prayer of Intercession

Intercession is standing in the gap for others. It is praying on behalf of people, nations, or situations beyond our own needs.

- **Scripture:** *"I exhort therefore, that, first of all, supplications, prayers, intercessions, and giving of thanks, be made for all men."* (1 Timothy 2:1).
- **Example:** Abraham interceded for Sodom; Moses interceded for Israel.
- **Application:** Make a prayer list of others—family, leaders, missionaries, the lost—and lift them up regularly.

Illustration: Intercession is like holding a rope for someone climbing a mountain—you are helping to secure their journey.

The Prayer of Agreement

Agreement multiplies the power of prayer. Jesus promised in Matthew 18:19: *"If two of you shall agree on earth as touching any thing that they shall ask, it shall be done for them of my Father which is in heaven."*

- **Example:** The early church prayed together in Acts 4, and the place was shaken with God's power.
- **Application:** Partner with fellow believers in prayer for needs too great to bear alone.

Illustration: Agreement in prayer is like several people pushing a stalled car together—the combined force moves what one person could not.

The Prayer of Spiritual Warfare

This type of prayer is aimed at resisting the enemy and advancing God's kingdom. It involves declaring God's authority, binding the works of darkness, and releasing His power.

- **Scripture:** *"For the weapons of our warfare are not carnal, but mighty through God to the pulling down of strong holds."* (2 Corinthians 10:4).
- **Example:** Paul prayed against demonic opposition hindering the gospel.
- **Application:** Put on the armor of God (Ephesians 6:10–18) and pray with authority in Jesus' name.

Illustration: Warfare prayer is like a soldier calling in air support. We are not fighting alone—heaven fights for us.

Practical Models of Prayer

1. **The ACTS Model** – Adoration, Confession, Thanksgiving, Supplication.
2. **The Lord's Prayer** – Worship, submission to God's will, daily needs, forgiveness, and deliverance (Matthew 6:9–13).
3. **Praying the Psalms** – Using Scripture itself as prayer.

The Beauty of Balance

If our prayer life only consists of asking (supplication), it becomes shallow. But when we add adoration, confession, thanksgiving, intercession, and spiritual warfare, our prayer life becomes rich and dynamic. Just as a balanced diet nourishes the body, a balanced prayer life nourishes the soul.

Reflection & Study Questions

1. Which type of prayer do you practice most often? Which do you practice least?
2. Why is it important to begin prayer with adoration before moving to requests?
3. Who are three people you can begin to intercede for daily?
4. How could you incorporate the ACTS model into your prayer routine this week?
5. Choose one type of prayer (adoration, confession, thanksgiving, supplication, intercession, agreement, or warfare) and spend 15 minutes practicing it today.

Chapter 8 – Prayer and Fasting

The Power of Combining Prayer with Fasting

Prayer alone is powerful. But when combined with fasting, it becomes a spiritual force that brings breakthrough. Fasting is the voluntary act of setting aside food—or other legitimate pleasures—for a spiritual purpose. It is not about punishing the body but about focusing the spirit.

Jesus Himself assumed His followers would fast. In Matthew 6:16 He said: *"Moreover when ye fast, be not, as the hypocrites, of a sad countenance..."* Notice He didn't say *if* you fast, but *when* you fast. This means fasting is not optional but expected in the life of a believer.

Biblical Foundations of Fasting

Throughout Scripture, men and women of God fasted in times of crisis, decision, repentance, or seeking revival.

- **Moses** fasted 40 days on Mount Sinai before receiving the Ten Commandments (Exodus 34:28).
- **David** fasted when seeking God's mercy (Psalm 35:13).
- **Esther** called a three-day fast before approaching the king, resulting in the deliverance of her people (Esther 4:16).
- **Daniel** fasted from choice foods as he sought understanding from God (Daniel 10:2–3).
- **Jesus** fasted 40 days in the wilderness before beginning His public ministry (Matthew 4:2).
- **The early church** fasted before sending missionaries and making major decisions (Acts 13:2–3).

In each case, fasting sharpened spiritual focus, humbled the heart, and released divine intervention.

What Fasting Is (and Is Not)

- **Fasting is:**
  - Abstaining from food (or certain foods) for a season to seek God.
  - A way of humbling ourselves before Him (Psalm 69:10).
  - A spiritual discipline that aligns us with God's will.
  - A way of intensifying prayer focus.
- **Fasting is not:**
  - A hunger strike to force God's hand.
  - A way to earn righteousness.
  - A public display of piety. Jesus warned against fasting to be seen by men (Matthew 6:16–18).

Why Prayer and Fasting Bring Breakthrough

1. **Fasting Humble Us** – It reminds us of our dependence on God.
2. **Fasting Clears Distractions** – By quieting the body, we sharpen spiritual sensitivity.
3. **Fasting Strengthens Prayer** – Ezra 8:23 says, *"So we fasted and besought our God for this: and he was intreated of us."*
4. **Fasting Brings Deliverance** – Jesus said some demons only come out by prayer and fasting (Mark 9:29).
5. **Fasting Prepares for New Assignments** – Before great missions, the early church fasted and prayed (Acts 13:2–3).

Types of Fasts

- **Complete Fast** – Abstaining from all food, drinking only water (as with Jesus and Moses).
- **Partial Fast** – Limiting certain foods or meals (like Daniel).
- **Corporate Fast** – A group fasting together for a shared purpose (like Esther and the Jews).

- **Personal Fast** – An individual seeking God privately.
- **Non-Food Fasts** – Abstaining from activities such as media or entertainment to seek God more intentionally.

Biblical and Historical Testimonies

- When **Nineveh** fasted and repented at Jonah's preaching, God withheld judgment (Jonah 3:5–10).
- During the **Great Revival of 1904 in Wales**, believers combined prayer with fasting, leading to a movement that spread worldwide.
- Modern missionaries and leaders testify that fasting opened doors, released provision, and broke spiritual strongholds.

Illustration

Think of fasting like sharpening an axe. A dull axe requires more effort and produces less result. Prayer without fasting is powerful, but sometimes dull through distractions. When we fast, we sharpen the edge of prayer, cutting more deeply into spiritual strongholds.

Practical Guidelines for Fasting

1. **Start Small** – Begin with a meal or a day. Build up gradually.
2. **Stay Hydrated** – Drink water and care for your health.
3. **Replace Meals with Prayer** – Don't just go hungry; spend the time with God.
4. **Use Scripture** – Read and meditate on God's Word during fasts.
5. **End Gradually** – Break the fast gently with light foods.

Reflection & Study Questions

1. What role has fasting played in your spiritual life so far?
2. Why do you think Jesus expected His followers to fast?

3. Which biblical example of fasting inspires you most—Moses, Esther, Daniel, or Jesus?
4. What distractions might God be calling you to set aside to seek Him more deeply?
5. Plan a fast this month (whether a meal, a day, or a partial fast). Journal your prayers and record how God meets you.

Chapter 9 – The Prayer of Agreement

The Power of United Prayer

There is something uniquely powerful about believers coming together in prayer. While individual prayer is essential, Scripture teaches that **corporate prayer carries multiplied power**. Jesus Himself promised in Matthew 18:19–20:

"Again I say unto you, That if two of you shall agree on earth as touching any thing that they shall ask, it shall be done for them of my Father which is in heaven. For where two or three are gathered together in my name, there am I in the midst of them."

This is the **prayer of agreement**—when believers unite their hearts and voices before God, heaven responds in a special way.

The Principle of Agreement

Agreement in prayer is not merely people praying at the same time. It is **unity of heart, faith, and purpose**.

- **Amos 3:3** asks: *"Can two walk together, except they be agreed?"* Agreement is more than words—it is alignment.
- Agreement means joining together in faith, not in doubt. If one person prays in faith and another in unbelief, there is no true agreement.
- Agreement also requires humility. It is not about one person's will, but about aligning together with God's will.

Biblical Examples of Agreement in Prayer

1. **The Early Church in Acts 1** – Before Pentecost, the disciples gathered *"with one accord in prayer and supplication"* (Acts 1:14). The Spirit was poured out on united believers.

2. The Church Praying for Peter – When Peter was in prison, the church prayed earnestly together (Acts 12:5). Their united prayer moved God to send an angel and set Peter free.

3. Jehoshaphat and Judah – Facing a massive army, King Jehoshaphat called the nation to fast and pray in agreement. God gave them victory without them lifting a sword (2 Chronicles 20:3–22).

4. The Multiplying Effect of Agreement

5. Deuteronomy 32:30 says: *"How should one chase a thousand, and two put ten thousand to flight..."* Agreement multiplies power. One believer's prayer is mighty, but united believers shake kingdoms of darkness.

6. **Illustration:** Think of one match—small but powerful. Two matches together create a bigger flame. But hundreds of matches ignited together can start a blazing fire that spreads uncontrollably. Agreement in prayer ignites spiritual fire.

Historical Testimonies of Agreement in Prayer

- **The Moravian Revival (1727):** A small group of believers agreed to begin a 24-hour prayer chain. That chain continued unbroken for 100 years and birthed a worldwide missionary movement.
- **The Second Great Awakening (1800s):** Groups of Christians gathered in homes and churches, agreeing together for revival. Their prayers ushered in one of the most powerful revivals in American history.
- **The Korean Church:** Known for its early morning prayer gatherings, thousands unite daily in agreement. This culture of

united prayer has fueled explosive church growth in South Korea.

Barriers to Agreement

For agreement to work, believers must guard against division. Jesus warned that *"Every kingdom divided against itself is brought to desolation."* (Matthew 12:25).

Common barriers include:

- Pride or competition.
- Doubt or unbelief.
- Hidden sin or unforgiveness.
- Distractions or lack of focus.

To experience true agreement, hearts must be clean, motives pure, and minds united in Christ.

How to Practice the Prayer of Agreement

1. **Find a Prayer Partner or Group** – Even two or three is enough for Jesus to be present.
2. **Agree on Scripture** – Base your prayer on God's promises to ensure alignment with His will.
3. **Pray with Unity and Faith** – Stand together, declaring God's Word boldly.
4. **Be Persistent** – Keep meeting and praying until the breakthrough comes.
5. **Celebrate Together** – When God answers, rejoice and give Him glory as a community.

Illustration

Imagine a heavy log too big for one person to move. Alone, it is impossible. But when several people put their hands together in the same direction, the log shifts easily. In the same way, united prayer moves what individual effort cannot.

Reflection & Study Questions

1. Why do you think Jesus placed such emphasis on agreement in prayer?
2. Can you recall a time when praying with others brought breakthrough that personal prayer alone did not?
3. What barriers to unity might be present in your relationships that could hinder agreement?
4. Who could you invite to join you in regular prayer of agreement?
5. This week, choose one specific request and pray it daily with at least one other believer. Record what God does.

Chapter 10 – Persistent Prayer

The Call to Persevere

One of the greatest lessons Jesus taught about prayer is the need for persistence. Luke 18:1 says: *"And he spake a parable unto them to this end, that men ought always to pray, and not to faint."*

Why did Jesus emphasize persistence? Because God delights in faith that refuses to quit. Persistence in prayer is not about overcoming God's reluctance—it is about laying hold of His willingness. It develops character, strengthens faith, and brings us into deeper dependence on Him.

The Parable of the Persistent Widow

In Luke 18:2–8, Jesus told of a widow who repeatedly came to an unjust judge, pleading for justice. Though he neither feared God nor cared about people, her persistence wore him down. Finally, he granted her request just to be rid of her.

Jesus contrasted this unjust judge with our heavenly Father. If persistence moved an ungodly man, how much more will our loving God respond to His chosen ones who cry out day and night? The lesson is clear: never stop praying.

Persistence in Scripture

- **Abraham** persisted in interceding for Sodom, bargaining with God down from fifty righteous to ten (Genesis 18:23–32).
- **Jacob** wrestled with the angel all night and declared, *"I will not let thee go, except thou bless me"* (Genesis 32:26).
- **Hannah** prayed year after year for a child until God answered (1 Samuel 1:12–20).
- **Elijah** prayed seven times for rain, sending his servant to look toward the sea until a small cloud appeared (1 Kings 18:42–44).

- **The Early Church** prayed continually for Peter in prison until the answer came (Acts 12:5).

These examples remind us: persistent prayer is the pathway to breakthrough.

Why Persistence Matters

1. **It Tests Our Faith** – Do we truly believe God will answer, or do we give up too easily?
2. **It Purifies Our Motives** – The longer we pray, the more our desires align with God's will.
3. **It Builds Endurance** – Persistence develops spiritual stamina.
4. **It Prepares the Answer** – Sometimes the delay is God aligning circumstances for His perfect timing.
5. **It Deepens Our Relationship** – Ongoing prayer keeps us close to the Father even before the answer arrives.

The Danger of Giving Up

Too often, believers quit praying right before the breakthrough. Galatians 6:9 reminds us: *"And let us not be weary in well doing: for in due season we shall reap, if we faint not."*

Giving up in prayer is like a miner quitting just inches from striking gold. We don't know how close we are to the answer—so we must keep pressing.

Historical and Modern Testimonies

- **George Müller** prayed for the salvation of five friends. The first came to Christ after five years, the next two after ten, the fourth after twenty-five, and the fifth after Müller's death. That last friend was saved at his funeral. Müller's persistence bore fruit across decades.
- **The Welsh Revival (1904)** was preceded by years of persistent

prayer from small groups who refused to give up despite spiritual dryness.

- Many parents testify of praying for prodigal children for years—even decades—until God brought them home.

Illustration

Persistent prayer is like water dripping on a rock. One drop may seem powerless, but over time the rock erodes and a hole is formed. Each prayer may feel small, but persistence wears down resistance and opens the way for God's answer.

How to Cultivate Persistence

1. **Set Prayer Goals** – Be specific about what you're believing God for.
2. **Pray Daily** – Make persistence part of your rhythm.
3. **Keep a Journal** – Record requests and track progress.
4. **Encourage Yourself with Scripture** – Stand on verses of promise.
5. **Refuse Discouragement** – When doubt whispers, declare God's faithfulness.
6. **Celebrate Small Signs** – Rejoice in partial answers as steps toward the full breakthrough.

Reflection & Study Questions

1. Have you ever given up praying for something too soon? What happened?
2. Which biblical example of persistence in prayer speaks most to your heart?
3. What request in your life requires long-term persistence right now?

4. How can you guard your heart against discouragement when answers delay?

5. This week, choose one persistent prayer request and commit to praying daily for 30 days. Journal your journey.

Chapter 11 – The Results of Prayer

Prayer Produces Fruit

God never calls His children to pray in vain. Every prayer sown in faith produces fruit. Sometimes the answer comes quickly; sometimes it comes slowly. Sometimes it comes in ways we did not expect. But one thing is certain: **prayer always produces results**—in us, in others, and in the world.

Isaiah 55:11 assures us: *"So shall my word be that goeth forth out of my mouth: it shall not return unto me void, but it shall accomplish that which I please, and it shall prosper in the thing whereto I sent it."* When our prayers align with God's Word, they cannot fail.

Prayer Brings Peace

Philippians 4:6–7 promises: *"Be careful for nothing; but in every thing by prayer and supplication with thanksgiving let your requests be made known unto God. And the peace of God, which passeth all understanding, shall keep your hearts and minds through Christ Jesus."*

The first result of prayer is often not external change, but internal peace. Even before the answer arrives, prayer lifts the burden and brings calm assurance.

- **Illustration:** Prayer is like transferring a heavy backpack from your shoulders onto God's. The load is lifted, and peace replaces anxiety.

Prayer Brings Strength

Isaiah 40:31 declares: *"They that wait upon the Lord shall renew their strength."* Prayer is the place of renewal. When Elijah was discouraged and ready to give up, he prayed, and God renewed his strength with food, rest, and divine encounter (1 Kings 19:4–8).

- **Example:** Jesus in Gethsemane prayed in agony, and an angel came to strengthen Him (Luke 22:43). Prayer gives us fresh endurance to face trials.

Prayer Brings Healing and Deliverance

James 5:14–15 teaches that the prayer of faith will heal the sick. Prayer has been God's instrument for physical, emotional, and spiritual healing throughout history.

- **Hezekiah** prayed for healing, and God added fifteen years to his life (2 Kings 20:1–6).
- Countless believers testify of miraculous healings and deliverances through prayer today.
- **Illustration:** Prayer is like medicine for the soul and body—administered by the Great Physician Himself.

Prayer Brings Provision

Jesus taught us to pray, *"Give us this day our daily bread."* (Matthew 6:11). God provides daily needs in response to prayer.

- **Elijah** was fed by ravens during famine (1 Kings 17:6).
- **George Müller's Orphanages** never lacked food though he never asked men—only God. Miraculously, bread and milk would arrive at the exact hour they were needed.

Prayer unlocks heaven's storehouse.

Prayer Brings Salvation

At its core, salvation itself begins with prayer. *"Whosoever shall call upon the name of the Lord shall be saved."* (Romans 10:13). Prayer also brings salvation to others as we intercede for the lost.

- **Example:** Cornelius, a Roman centurion, prayed faithfully. His prayers brought angelic visitation and the salvation of his household (Acts 10:1–48).
- History is full of mothers, fathers, and grandparents who prayed their children and grandchildren into the Kingdom.

Prayer Brings Revival

No revival in history has ever begun without prayer. When God's people humble themselves and pray, heaven responds (2 Chronicles 7:14).

- **The First Great Awakening (1700s):** Sparked by prayer meetings across Europe and America.
- **The Welsh Revival (1904):** Born from persistent intercession of a few faithful saints.
- **The Azusa Street Revival (1906):** Prayer meetings in Los Angeles ignited a Pentecostal movement that swept the globe.

Prayer shakes nations.

Prayer Brings Victory Over the Enemy

Prayer is a weapon of warfare. Through it, strongholds are torn down, demons are cast out, and Satan's plans are defeated.

- **Daniel** prayed, and angelic armies warred in the heavenly realms to deliver his answer (Daniel 10:12–13).
- **Paul and Silas** prayed and sang hymns in prison; chains broke, doors opened, and captives were set free (Acts 16:25–26).

Prayer does not just protect us—it defeats the enemy's schemes.

Why Some Results Delay

Sometimes we pray and do not see immediate results. This does not mean prayer is wasted. God may be:

- **Testing our faith** – Will we keep trusting Him?
- **Purifying our motives** – Are we praying for His glory or our gain?
- **Arranging circumstances** – Aligning people and events for His perfect timing.
- **Working in unseen ways** – Just as seeds grow underground

before sprouting, answers often develop invisibly before appearing.

Illustration

Prayer is like planting seeds in a garden. Some sprout quickly; others take weeks or months. But if you keep watering and waiting, the harvest always comes.

Reflection & Study Questions

1. Which of the results of prayer (peace, strength, healing, provision, salvation, revival, victory) have you personally experienced?
2. How has prayer brought peace to your heart in the middle of trials?
3. Do you have a testimony where prayer produced an unexpected result in your life?
4. What area of your life right now needs the results of persistent prayer?
5. This week, choose one of these results and focus your prayers specifically on that area. Record what God does.

Chapter 12 – Living a Lifestyle of Prayer

Beyond Occasional Prayer

For many believers, prayer is an event—something reserved for church services, meal times, or moments of crisis. But the Bible calls us to something much deeper: **a lifestyle of prayer.**

Paul exhorts in 1 Thessalonians 5:17: *"Pray without ceasing."* This does not mean speaking words nonstop every hour of the day. It means cultivating a continual awareness of God's presence, living in constant communion with Him. Prayer is not meant to be a part of life—it is meant to be the atmosphere of life.

What Does It Mean to "Pray Without Ceasing"?

1. **Continual Connection** – Like a phone call that never ends, our hearts stay connected to God throughout the day.
2. **An Attitude of Dependence** – Prayer becomes the default response to every challenge, joy, or decision.
3. **Awareness of God's Presence** – Living each moment mindful that He is with us.
4. **Spontaneous Conversation** – Whispering prayers while walking, driving, or working.

Jesus: A Life of Prayer

Jesus modeled prayer as a lifestyle. He prayed in the morning, evening, before meals, before decisions, in times of joy, in times of sorrow, and even in His final breath. Prayer was not an event for Him—it was the rhythm of His life.

If the Son of God needed to live in constant prayer, so do we.

The Benefits of a Lifestyle of Prayer

1. **Closeness with God** – Prayer deepens intimacy, making us

more sensitive to His voice.

2. **Guidance for Daily Living** – The Spirit directs decisions when we live in constant communion.
3. **Peace and Joy** – Anxiety decreases when every burden is immediately brought to the Lord.
4. **Strength to Resist Temptation** – Jesus told His disciples, *"Watch and pray, that ye enter not into temptation"* (Matthew 26:41).
5. **Fruitfulness in Ministry** – Lasting impact flows from a prayer-saturated life.

Hindrances to a Lifestyle of Prayer

1. **Busyness** – Filling schedules so full that prayer is crowded out.
2. **Distractions** – Technology, entertainment, and noise that steal focus.
3. **Compartmentalization** – Treating prayer as something for "church time" rather than daily life.
4. **Lack of Discipline** – Neglecting the habit of setting aside time for God.

Practical Ways to Develop a Prayer Lifestyle

1. **Morning Devotion** – Begin each day with prayer and Scripture.
2. **Breath Prayers** – Simple prayers whispered throughout the day (e.g., "Lord, guide me," "Thank You, Jesus").
3. **Prayer Walks** – Turn walks into times of intercession for your neighborhood.
4. **Prayer Journaling** – Record prayers and answers to see God's faithfulness.
5. **Family Prayer** – Make prayer part of meals, bedtime, and family decisions.

6. **Corporate Prayer** – Join a prayer group at church or with friends.
7. **End the Day with God** – Reflect in prayer before sleep, giving thanks and surrendering tomorrow.

Illustration

A lifestyle of prayer is like breathing. You don't only breathe when you're in trouble—you breathe constantly. In the same way, prayer should be as natural and continual as breathing, sustaining our spiritual life.

Historical and Modern Examples

- **Brother Lawrence**, a humble monk in the 1600s, wrote *The Practice of the Presence of God*. He lived in constant prayer, even while washing dishes, turning every act into worship.
- **Smith Wigglesworth** said he rarely prayed longer than half an hour, but he never went half an hour without praying. His entire life became saturated with prayer.
- Many modern believers testify that living in constant prayer turns ordinary tasks into sacred encounters.

The Goal: Becoming a House of Prayer

God's vision for His people is clear: *"My house shall be called a house of prayer for all people."* (Isaiah 56:7). This is not just about church buildings—it's about us. We are the temple of the Holy Spirit (1 Corinthians 6:19). Our lives should radiate prayer as our defining characteristic.

Reflection & Study Questions

1. What does "pray without ceasing" mean to you personally?
2. What daily distractions most often pull you away from prayer?
3. Which of the practical steps listed could you begin implementing this week?

4. How can you cultivate an awareness of God's presence in ordinary activities like work, chores, or driving?

5. Write a short "breath prayer" you can carry throughout the week, repeating it whenever you think of God.

Conclusion – A Call to Prayer

The Church's Greatest Need

Across history, nations have risen and fallen, empires have come and gone, but one truth has remained: God moves in response to the prayers of His people. More than programs, strategies, or innovations, the greatest need of the church today is a return to **prayer**.

Leonard Ravenhill once said: *"No man is greater than his prayer life."* Likewise, no church is greater than its collective prayer life. We can preach eloquent sermons, organize activities, and fill calendars—but without prayer, we are powerless.

Prayer Shapes History

- It was prayer that closed the mouths of lions in Daniel's day.
- It was prayer that brought fire down on Mount Carmel through Elijah.
- It was prayer that birthed the church on the Day of Pentecost.
- It was prayer that set prisoners free at midnight in Philippi.

If prayer shaped history then, it can shape history now. God is still the same yesterday, today, and forever (Hebrews 13:8).

A Call to the Individual

You, child of God, are called to be a person of prayer. Do not think prayer is only for pastors, prophets, or "spiritual elites." Prayer is the inheritance of every believer. James 5:17 reminds us that Elijah was a man *"subject to like passions as we are"*—he was human like us. Yet his prayers shut the heavens and opened them again.

If Elijah could pray with such effect, so can you.

A Call to Families

Families must return to the altar of prayer. In many homes, television and technology have replaced family prayer. But the strongest families are those built on the foundation of united prayer. Parents who pray with their children plant seeds of faith that will outlast generations.

A Call to Churches

The early church was born in a prayer meeting, not a planning meeting (Acts 1:14). The fire of Pentecost fell on believers gathered in unity and prayer. Today's churches must return to that upper-room posture.

Churches that pray will see revival. Churches that neglect prayer will wither. Prayer must not be a side ministry but the heartbeat of the body.

A Call to Nations

2 Chronicles 7:14 gives us God's condition for national healing:

"If my people, which are called by my name, shall humble themselves, and pray, and seek my face, and turn from their wicked ways; then will I hear from heaven, and will forgive their sin, and will heal their land."

The healing of nations begins not in parliaments or palaces, but in prayer closets and church altars.

Prayer as Revival Fire

Every great revival has been birthed in prayer, and every revival dies when prayer ceases. If we long for the glory of God to cover the earth, then we must be willing to bend our knees.

Prayer is not preparation for the battle—it **is** the battle. When the church prays, darkness trembles, heaven rejoices, and the Kingdom advances.

Your Invitation

This book has shown what prayer is, why it is powerful, how Jesus modeled it, how the Spirit empowers it, and how persistence, faith, fasting, agreement, and a lifestyle of prayer bring transformation. But now, the responsibility rests with you.

Will prayer be a casual activity, or will it become the defining rhythm of your life? Will you be a spectator, or will you be an intercessor?

Final Exhortation

Rise up, prayer warrior. Your prayers matter. They ascend like incense before the throne of God (Revelation 5:8). They shake strongholds, save souls, and change destinies.

Heaven is waiting. The world is groaning. God is listening.

So pray—pray with faith, pray with persistence, pray with fire, pray until heaven invades earth.

For information, permissions, or inquiries, please contact:
Dr. Greg Wood
P.O. Box 240
Pharr, Texas 78577
info@fountainoflifemx.org
ISBN: 979-8-90046-106-9
Printed in USA
First Edition – 2025

Prayer is a profund' impact that a Jubiant grown in the Life of a Christian is, the importance of divine strength, and draws us closer to God–to almost spiritual sense.

Learn–how to examine your prayer life through:

- Understanding the nature and purpose of prayer
- Developing a consistent and meaningful prayer practice
- Experiencing the various dimensions of prayer, from adoration and confession to thanksgiving and supplica-
- Witnessing the impact of prayer on individual lives and the world

Let in look to intimathe life-changing power of prayer— a deeper intimacy with God. and lujen, forward in an impretituoous power with God.

Don't miss out!

Visit the website below and you can sign up to receive emails whenever Dr. Greg Wood publishes a new book. There's no charge and no obligation.

https://books2read.com/r/B-A-GGWME-MVFWG

BOOKS 2 READ

Connecting independent readers to independent writers.

Also by Dr. Greg Wood

Praise and Worship
EL PODER DE LA ORACION
The Power of Prayer
Empoderados
El Orden Cronológico de los Tiempos del Fin
The Chronological Order of the End Times
Principios de Consejería Noutético
The Principles of Nouthetic Counseling
Alabanza y Adoración
Liderazgo